Inspired

By

The Light

Inspired

By

The Light

by Hannah Lee Liles

Jacket Design by Sunflower Publishing Company

Printed in the United States of America
        By Jostens Graphics

        Published by
SUNFLOWER PUBLISHING COMPANY
P.O. Box 240602
Charlotte, North Carolina 28224

A Note From The Pastor
ʕ୫୪୰୪ୣଵ

It's not often that one has the opportunity to share in a dream. However, from the first moment I heard Hannah Liles say that "God has given me a special gift to write poetry," I knew that it would not be long before Hannah would step out in faith with this project. That's Hannah, determined, bold, courageous and full of faith. Most of all she loves God and her lifestyle is reflected in her writings.

I met Hannah Liles in 1990 at the church where I pastor. A mutual bond of respect and friendship developed between us almost immediately. I saw Hannah as my daughter and was determined that she would learn the Word of God and serve God faithfully. Hannah did not need much encouragement, because she came to Nations Ford Baptist Church of Charlotte, with a willing heart and a teachable spirit. It is no surprise to me that she matured in the faith so quickly and that she could clearly hear the voice of God calling her to inspire others through the light of poetry.

As I read this work, I could truly sense the presence of God's warm embrace. Jesus said that "we are the light of the world," and I believe that Hannah Liles' light will shine for many years to come. This I believe is just the beginning of a great work of inspiration and encouragement that God will produce through Sister Hannah Liles. She is truly a chosen vessel and has come into the kingdom for such a time as this.

&ଔଔ&

    Thank you Hannah for being obedient to that "heavenly vision" and for you pouring out your heart to be a blessing to the Body of Christ. It is my hope that God will use "Inspired By The Light," to not only encourage the believers, but to win the unbelievers to Jesus Christ.

Rev. Phillips M. Davis, Senior Pastor
Nations Ford Baptist Church

Contents

PART ONE

PART TWO

PART THREE

Acknowledgements
❧❦❧

This book is dedicated first to God, my best friend. I am thankful and humbled by the talents, blessings, love, grace and opportunities He has given me.

To my family, it is my desire that you will be inspired by reading this book of inspirational poems. This book is my testimony that putting God first is a prerequisite for success in all areas of my life.

To my family and friends, I thank each person from my heart, for your prayers, encouraging words, and generous support all during this past year. Thank you for giving me your listening ear. Whatever your task was during the time I wrote this book, I really appreciate all your help. You are my angels.

Special thanks to Valeria Wallace and Lois Osborne for planting vision seeds.

Special thanks to Timothy Gibbs, Daisy Love and Barbara Lawing, who edited the text. I really do appreciate all your help from my heart.

Special thanks to Ed Bohannon and Shirley Moore for all your help.

Special thanks to my Pastor, Dr. Phillip M. Davis. Thank you for believing in me as a sister in Christ, and as a writer.

Why I Wrote This Book

This book is for anyone who needs and wants a best friend. I pray as you read these words of hope and encouragement, you come to know and trust God. I pray that you will be inspired to become intimate with God. When the Holy Spirit touches my heart to write about something, it may be while driving to or from work, reading a book, sitting under the hair dryer, listening to the radio, watching inspirational television, or talking to a friend. I never know when I will be inspired to write. I can walk by someone and hear a word or two of a conversation and be led by the Holy Spirit to write an inspirational poem.

I am single and love God more than anybody else in this whole wide world. Just thinking about God or hearing His name, I start smiling. Happy tears fill my eyes, because I know God is with me at all times. I just want someone else to experience the joy that I have with my best friend, Jesus. When things happen in my life, minor problems or something major, I pray and ask God, "What should I do about this situation?" My God has all the answers for any situation I come in contact with.

Yes, I am human, and I make mistakes. But I believe in miracles, believe in the impossible. God will turn a situation around when we ask for His help. Look at me and you see proof of that.

God gives us what is best for us when we yield our hearts to Him.

Try my best friend Jesus and see for yourself. I pray that the power of God will unfold in your life from this day until eternity.

Scripture verses I meditated on while writing this book are from the King James version of the Holy Bible, Old and New Testaments, and are as follows:

Matthew 6:33
But seek ye first the kingdom of God, and his righteousness; and all these things shall be added unto you.

Proverbs 29:18
Where there is no vision, the people perish: but he that keepeth the law, happy is he.

Proverbs 3:5, 6
Trust in the Lord with all thine heart; and lean not unto thine own understanding. In all thy ways acknowledge him, and he shall direct thy paths.

Psalm 139:23, 24
Search me, O God, and know my heart: try me, and know my thoughts. And see if there be any wicked way in me, and lead me in the way everlasting.

Introduction

∽ཉ℘ཉℳ

I walk into my bedroom and start to go to the closet but instead I walk over to my bathroom and see this light shining on the wall. I walk over to the light. My eyes follow this light outside my bedroom window. I see a big, full moon looking at me. I whisper, "Oh, God, I've got to tell somebody." I pick up the telephone and call my friend Donna, but she isn't home. I call another friend and tell him he has to go to his kitchen window and look out to see this moon. He tells me he is on a long distance telephone call and will call me back. I tell him I don't want him to call me back, I just want him to go look out his window and see this moon because it's huge.

I hang up the telephone and look at this moon and say, "God, every time I try to tell someone about your goodness, there's no one around to tell." I just stand there looking. I sense the presence of God saying to me, "I will listen to you, talk to me, tell me what's on your mind, I will always be here for you."

I walk back into my living room and sit on the couch and pick up a note pad and write what happened. I write the poem called "The Moon."

My friend Emily calls, and I tell her what just happened. I read the poem to her. She says it is awesome. Emily says she didn't know I was a poet. I say, "what. . . . I didn't know I was a poet either." Emily shares with me that she writes poems too. Emily and I talk further, but I don't say anything about the notion of being a poet. I am at a loss for words.

The next day at work, Monday, October 9, 1995, I type this poem "The Moon" and I send it via E-mail to a couple of my friends and pass it around the office. Everyone tells me they like it, that it's "deep." My friends want me to make them copies they can keep. My friends ask me what newspaper or magazine I got it out of. I tell them "Hannah's book."

On Wednesday, some of my co-workers and I go to First Baptist Church for lunch and worship service. Dr. Charles Page, Pastor of the church, says "Did anyone see the full moon last night? It was awesome." Sandra, my co-worker says, "Yes, Hannah had a wake up call last night."

I go to Bible Study Wednesday night and tell my Praise and Worship class what happened to me Sunday night. I read the class several poems written since then. My class members tell me that it's a miracle from God. You see, I'd never written any poems nor had anything like this happen to me before.

Two of my class members, Sister Yvonne and Sister Mary, look at each other and say, "She's going to be the next Helen Steiner Rice." I tell my class members with excitement in my voice and a gleam in my eyes that I will write a book, inspirational cards, and do other things in the future with my poems. I tell my class members I give God all the glory.

Part One

Intimacy With God

⚜️

Wake Up Call

God stopped by my house and gave
me a wake up call. God shared with
me what he wanted me to do.

I am to use my writing skills to
spread the Gospel of Jesus around the
world in books, cards, and songs.

Thank you, God, for stopping by my
house and giving me a wake up call
to do your will.

I am glad I was listening for your whisper.

God's calling you to do His desire.
Are you listening?

*"I will instruct thee and teach thee in the way which thou
shalt go: I will guide thee with mine eye."
Psalm 32:8*

What Is A Friend?

⊰⧓⧓⊱

A friend is a person who will
tell you the truth no matter
what you want to hear.

A friend is a person you can
trust with your most important
secrets, and not worry about
hearing them from someone else.

God never repeats your secrets
to anyone. Most of all, God's
telephone number is never busy.
That's what I call a friend.

"A man that hath friends must show himself friendly:
and there is a friend that sticketh closer than a brother."
Proverbs 18:24

Jesus Is My Best Friend

⋘🙐🙐⋙

When I came home today, just for a
minute I took my eyes off Him. I was sad,
hurt and lonely because you did not call.
You see, I just wanted to hear your voice.
You said you were my friend.

I remembered my best friend, "Jesus, Jesus."
Jesus said He will always be there for me
no matter what I go through.

I can call Him anytime, anywhere and
hear His voice.

He turns my sadness, hurt and loneliness
into happiness.

You see, friend, I put my eyes back on
"Jesus, Jesus" by praising Him, thanking
Him and telling Him that I love Him more
than anybody else in this whole wide world.

*"Jesus saith unto him, I am the way, the truth,
and the life: no man cometh unto the Father,
but by me."*
John 14:6

Thank You

❧ಬಬ❧

How many times in our lives
have we just wanted to say,
Thank you, Heavenly Father,
for giving us the gifts of the day?

Thank you, Heavenly Father,
for giving us inspirational
words we can share with others.

How many times in our lives
have we wanted to say
Thank You, Heavenly Father?
Something else caught our attention,
and we put it aside until later.
When something happens in our life,
who is the first person we call on?

*"O give thanks unto the Lord; for he is
good: for his mercy endureth forever."*
Psalm 136:1

6

Chosen By God

❧ ⅏ ⅏ ❧

I am chosen by God, to do this
task at this time in my life.
I don't know why God decided He
wanted me to do the things He
chose for me to do.

Thank you, God, for molding me
into the person you want me to be.

I cherish you, God, for choosing
me for this assignment.

I yield my heart only to God, for
the things God has chosen for me
to enjoy each and everyday
of my life.

*"As for God, His way is perfect: the word
of the Lord is tried: He is a buckler to all
those that trust in Him."*
Psalm 18:30

My Gift To you

❧🙠🙠❧

I came home today and went into my
quiet room. For a minute, I just stood
at the doorway, thanking God for the
gifts He has given me.

Most of all, the ability to share with
someone how God blesses me everyday.

Tears began to flow out of my eyes.
I felt the presence of God in the room
with me. I thanked God again for
blessing me with the ability to share
with someone through words of
encouragement, by sending a card or
picking up the telephone and sharing
some good news.

God has laid it upon my heart today
to tell you, you are his precious,
precious child. He is always there
for you. No matter what you are
going through, Jesus loves you.

This is my gift to you today.

*"But my God shall supply all your needs
according to his riches in glory by Christ Jesus."
Philippians 4:19*

The Gift

❧❧❧❧

I visited my friend today at the
convalescent home. She was so
happy to see me. She had this glow
on her face that brought a smile to
my face. Every time I think of her,
I praise God for her friendship.

I was going to give her a smile, but
instead she gave me the smile that I
so desperately needed today.

I took her a gift today, but instead
I received a gift from her that will
last a lifetime.

*"Let your light so shine before men, that
they may see your good works and glorify
your Father which is in heaven."*
Matthew 5:16

Strong Vessel

Thank you, God, for allowing me
to apply my writing skills, which
I thought was my weaker vessel.
Oh God, you turned this weak
vessel into a strong vessel.

God, I give you all the praise at
all times. Thank you, God,
for giving me the faith,
courage, and boldness
to do what you want
me to do with my vessel.

Whatever our weakness may be,
God is the answer. Always
remember that you can ask
God to turn your weakness into
your strength, anytime, anywhere
and any place. Thank you, God.
I give You all the praise.

"Trust in the Lord with all thine heart;
and lean not unto thine own understanding."
Proverbs 3:5

Powerless

◈❧❧◈

Most of all, God, you trusted me to
stand on Your word. Please, God,
forgive me as I forgive myself for
all my sins. Oh God, I am unhappy
because I let you down today.
God, I need your strength, direction
and peace.

Lord, thank you for touching my heart,
and letting me know that the reason why
I go through some things is to be a
stronger person.

For a moment, I felt helpless, but your
Spirit, God, took control over my mind,
body and soul. I felt powerless, and I
remembered the words, "Lord, help me."
Thank you, God. You came through as
always with your power and strength.
I love you dearly with all my heart.

"Then came she and worshipped him,
saying, Lord, help me."
Matthew 15:25

Have An Intimate
Talk With God

❧ ಶಿ ಶಿ ❧

Take off your shoes and
sit down. Have an intimate
talk with God today.

Be yourself and
let your hair down.
God wants us to relax and
enjoy His company.

"For thou shalt worship no other god:
for the Lord, whose name is Jealous,
is a jealous God."
Exodus 34:14

Quiet Time With God

◅৪৩৪৩◅

Lord, Lord, what do I tell my friend?
The one who lost her loved one?
God, she is sad. I feel her pain.
Her heart is broken to pieces. I know
she can put her trust in you, Lord. I
know you will heal her broken heart.
I know You will strengthen and direct
her, even in her sorrow.

God, I will remind her to hold your
hand tighter and tighter each day, and
keep her eyes on You at all times. I
know that You will bring her out of
this to be a stronger person than she is
right now, even in her sorrow.

"In my distress I cried unto the Lord, and he heard me."
Psalm 120:1

I Believe

❧❧❧

I can do all things through
Jesus who strengthens me.
I believe in God Almighty.
I know my God can do all things.
Yes, I believe in miracles because
my miracle is seeing my book and
inspirational cards published, and
hearing my songs on the radio.
Yes, this is what I believe in.

When I think how powerful God is,
happy tears come to my eyes.
This feeling that comes over me is
very powerful and I know that only
my God can make miracles happen.

My God is awesome, has all the
power! Believe in yourself,
continue to do God's will, stay
focused, and you will
be a success in God's eyes.

"And all things, whatsoever ye shall ask in
prayer, believing, ye shall receive."
Matthew 21:22

Intoxicated On God

જ8980જ

I get intoxicated on God by studying His word.

I don't worry about driving down the highway
being intoxicated on God's words,
and having a hangover the next morning.

I don't need alcohol or drugs to relax
and have fun or feel good.

I am fully committed to you, Lord.
Thank you, God, for letting me get
intoxicated on the Holy Spirit.

I don't worry about driving while
impaired and getting stopped
by a policeman.

When I take a drink from God's bottle
I always relax, feel good and have fun
when I am intoxicated on Him.

"But seek ye first the kingdom of God, and his
righteousness; and all these things shall be
added unto you."
Matthew 6:33

15

Your Word

❧ ಐ ಐ ❧

Your word is important.
When you tell someone
you're going to do something,
stand on your word. Your word
is the only thing you have
that remains with you forever.

God, I am glad you are not like us.
I am glad you stand behind your
word. Your word never changes
from day to day.

"But the word of the Lord endureth forever.
And this is the word which by the gospel is
preached unto you."
I Peter 1:25

Lunch With My Buddies

❦ℰℬℰ❦

I am excited about visiting
my little lunch buddies this week.

I wonder if my lunch buddies have
a relationship with Jesus?

I will introduce my lunch buddies
to my best friend, Jesus, if they
don't know Him.

Do your lunch buddies know Jesus?

*"A man that hath friends must show himself
friendly: and there is a friend that sticketh
closer than a brother."*
Proverbs 18:24

Attitude

⚜⚜⚜

Do you have an attitude
problem today?

Be still for one moment,
give your attitude to God
and he will fix it for you.

*"My help cometh from the Lord, which
made heaven and earth."*
Psalm 121:2

Color Of My Skin

Thank you, God, for not judging me on the
Color of my Skin. God, I am glad you are
looking at my heart.

Sometime others judge me by the color of
my skin. In what I can do or where I can
go, what kind of job I have or what kind of
house I live in, the car I drive or the clothes
I wear.

God, I am glad my skin color is not important
to You.

Thank you, God, for dying for me. You didn't
see any color in my skin when you were bleeding
on the cross for all of my sins. Praise God. . . .

God, You said, when I keep my mind focused on
you "I can do all things through Christ Jesus."
When I think of the color of my skin, I will
remember God doesn't see any skin color at all
when He looks at me.

*"For there is no difference between the Jew and
the Greek: for the same Lord overall is rich unto
all that call upon him."*
Romans 10:12

Looking In My Mirror

I looked up to see my eyes in the rear view mirror
as I backed out of my driveway this morning.
There was no mirror. The mirror had fallen,
and I couldn't see behind me.

When you can't see Jesus in your life,
others cannot see Him either.

As I was crossing three lanes of traffic without a
mirror, I could not see out of my car's back
window. I prayed and thanked God for being
my eyes.

Looking in this window this morning I could not
see my eyes, the reflection of Jesus. I felt lost
without seeing the reflection of Jesus in this
mirror with me. Jesus is in my heart even though
I could not see Him in the mirror this morning.
Now I understand, God, when you said let your
light shine before all men at all times.

Jesus lives within my heart daily. I put my
mirror back up again in my car. Now I can see
the reflection of Jesus in my car mirror again.
Thank you, Jesus for being my eyes.

*"Ye are the light of the world. A city that
is set on an hill cannot be hid."
Matthew 5:14*

Be Yourself

⊰⦵⦵⊰

God wants you to be yourself at
all times. Do not pretend to be
somebody you are not, because
you want others to love you.

Love yourself first.

Take off the mask and be real.

God can see through the mask
you are wearing. Be yourself,
because God knows your heart,
and every thought and dream.

*"Let your conversation be without
covetousness; and be content with
such things as ye have: for he hath
said, I will never leave thee, nor
forsake thee."*
Hebrews 13:5

You Are Special

❈❈❈❈

You are special and I love you.

God's children are special to Him.
When things don't go your way,
always remember Jesus loves you.
What people think or say to you or
about you is really not important.

What God thinks about you
is very important.

You have a special gift that God
gave to you, and no one else can
take it away from you.

We are all different in our own
special way.

Remember, you are always
special in God's eyes.

"Let not your heart be troubled; ye
believe in God, believe also in me."
John 14:1

Key To God's Heart

God has the key
to your heart.

If you want to get
in God's kingdom,
ask God for the key
to His heart.

"In my distress I cried unto the Lord,
and he heard me."
Psalm 120:1

Having A Relationship With God

Some people go to church all their life and still
don't know God. Some people don't have a
relationship with Him.

Get to know God like you know your friends or
family. Talk to God the same way. God always
has a listening ear and He will show you in His
Word what you should do for every situation
in your life.

You can make God Lord over your life, right now.
You can ask God to forgive you for all your sins
and wash you clean in the blood of Jesus.
God will forgive you only if you ask Him.
It's that simple, yes, open your mouth and tell God
that you believe in your heart that He died on
the cross for all your sins and He will be Lord
over your life.

God will do the rest if you believe in Him without
a doubt. You will be saved when you call upon the
name of the Lord. This is God's promise to you if
you accept Jesus as Lord. He will accept you
when you call upon His name and pray this prayer:

≈ಖಖ≈

Dear God, I know that I have sinned by breaking
your laws, and I ask for your forgiveness. I believe
that Jesus died for my sins. I want to be born again
and receive new life in You. Yes, I will follow Jesus
as my Lord and obey Him in all that I do. In the
name of Jesus I pray. Amen, Amen.

*"For whosoever shall call upon the name of the
Lord shall be saved."*
Romans 10:13

God's Star

❧☙☙❧

In Jesus' eyes, I am His Star.

I need you all to buy God's book
so we can spread the Gospel of Jesus
around the world.

You can be God's star by studying
His Word and doing His will.

God is my star.

Let God be your star.

"The Lord is my light and my salvation; whom shall I fear? The Lord is the strength of my life; of whom shall I be afraid?"
Psalm 27:1

Joy

❧ℰℰ℘ℰ℘ℰ❧

Joy comes from inside
your heart.
No one can give it to you
except God Almighty.

If you are unhappy
whose fault is it?

Call on Jesus today,
and ask Him to fill you
with the real joy that
last a lifetime.

"They that sow in tears shall reap in joy."
Psalm 126:5

Happy Anniversary To You

க்ஜூஜூக்

It's that time again - our anniversary.
This day will be special because when my eyes
met yours, I was in love with you from that day -
and love you more today than when we first met.

Thank you, God, I am glad You made only
one special person for me, and that
special person is You.

Happy Anniversary Always

*"Let love be without dissimulation. Abhor that
which is evil; cleave to that which is good."*
Romans 12:9

Today

Today I have so much
to be thankful for:
life, health, strength.
I have a home to
rest my head, food to eat,
and clothes to wear.

Today I want to say
thank you, God, for
letting me smell the
fresh air, and for letting
me see the sunshine
one more day.

*"Rejoice in the Lord, O ye righteous:
for praise is comely for the upright."*
Psalm 33:1

Part Two

Adversity - Life's Common Experiences

Facing My Fear

◈ৎৡৎৡৎ◈

Today is the day I will face this fear.
I began to pray to God, thanking Him
for helping me face this fear of driving
on this bridge.

God, the closer I get to this bridge my
heart is pounding faster, my stomach is bubbling,
my legs are shaking, I am trying to keep my foot
on the gas.

I take a deep breath, as I begin to drive slowly
up the ramp. I feel the presence of God saying to me,
"Fear not my child, I am with you." I begin to feel
better while driving on this bridge. Repeating to
myself God is with me, Jesus loves me, it's going
to be alright, I can drive on this bridge today.
All the way across this bridge I talked, and prayed
to God, the whole time.

When I reached the other side of this bridge,
I was back on solid ground. I stopped the car,
got out, looked back and said, "Thank you, God."
I faced my fear today, and now I can smile
when I drive on this bridge.

God wants us to give him all our fears, and he will
carry us through each one of them.

*"Fear not, little flock; for it is your Father's good
pleasure to give you the kingdom."*
Luke 12:32

33

Going Home To Be With My Heavenly Father

Let me go home to be with my Heavenly Father,
no more pains, no more tears.
I just want to go home
to be with my Heavenly Father.

I have served my time here on this earth
with you all, so, let me go home
to be with my Heavenly Father.

I am happy, I am free as a dove,
I am at peace with myself, so let me go home
to be with my Heavenly Father.

No more pains, no more tears for
my family and friends. I love you all dearly,
but it's time to say, I will see you all in Heaven
with my Heavenly Father.

Let me go in peace and enjoy the sunshine
with my Heavenly Father today.

Peace I leave you this glorious morning.

*"And God shall wipe away all tears from their
eyes; and there shall be no more death neither
sorrow, nor crying, neither shall there be any
more pain: for the former things are passed away."
Revelation 21:4*

I Feel Good Today

ఆ౬౬ఆ

Looking out my window today, I saw bright sunshine,
pale green grass, a tree leaning to one side. It is cool
outside. Fall has begun to settle in.

I need to put some pine needles around my trees
and shrubs, and plant some flowers for springtime.

Friends I called do not have the time to help me
without charging me a fee. If I had the money, I
would hire a landscaper to do my yard work.

I begin to pray. God, what shall I do about my yard
work? The answer came. I went to the store, bought
my pine needles, straightened my tree, planted some
flowers, and put fertilizer on my pale green grass.

Thanks again, Lord. I can and will depend on you for
direction, friendship and a listening ear, and most of
all Lord, you will not charge me a fee for helping me
do my yard work.

I feel good today looking out my window with a smile
and seeing that my yard work is done.

"The Lord will give strength unto his people."
Psalm 29:11

35

I Did Not Stop By
To Complain Today

Lord, do I come to you only when I want
to complain about something?

I am truly sorry, God; I want to
come to you anytime, anywhere with
good or bad news to share with you.

I am not here to complain today.
I just want to say I love you.
Thank you, God, for being so
understanding toward me.

I did not stop by to complain, just
wanted to say I'm happy with the
work you've given me to do. I am
going to tell everybody all over the
world about You and what you have
done for me. I will continue to praise,
praise your holy name, God Almighty.

*"This is the day which the Lord hath made;
we will rejoice and be glad in it."*
Psalm 118:24

In The Mood

⊰☙☙⊱

When you came home today
you checked your telephone
calls and your mail. You saw a
note from me. You put it aside
until later, because you didn't
want to hear from me today.

Sometimes we just do not want to
hear from God because we are
not in the mood to talk or listen
to Him today.

God does not have to be in the mood
to open His heart to us. I am so glad
God is not like me.

"Now we know that God heareth not sinners:
but if any man be a worshipper of God, and
doeth his will, him he heareth."
John 9:31

I Love You Lord

❧☙☙❧

I love you, Lord. Love you
in the midst of my job problems,
car problems, family problems -
even when I am not feeling very
well, I still love You, Lord.

In the midst of all these burdens,
I will keep focused on You, Lord.

Lord, you are holy and awesome in
your name. I just feel your love all
around me even in the midst of
my trials.

*"I love them that love me; and those
that seek me early shall find me."*
Proverbs 8:17

Car To The Shop

❧❀❀❧

I took my car to the shop again, Lord.
I feel like I am being taken advantage of
because I am a woman.

I told the serviceman that he is overcharging
me because I am a woman.

The serviceman said, "No ma'am,
I am just doing my job."

"Lord," I asked, "why should I go through
this again with this man?" If only I had a
knowledgeable man to take my car to the
shop, this serviceman would not charge me
these high prices.

Thank you, Lord, for reminding me to be
thankful I have a car to take to the shop.
I Thank You with a smile.

*"My brethren, count it all joy when ye fall
into divers temptations."*
James 1:2

There Is Hope

I was looking at my car today. I felt a glimmer
of hope that it will survive. There was no power
source in it.

The serviceman was holding part of this power
source in his hands. My car had a glow that
told me there was hope. It was not ready to
leave me yet.

Looking at our hearts, we sometimes
need to be revived, and washed in the
blood of Jesus.

Just like my car needed a new power source.
Sometimes we have to purge our hearts
and start over again.

There is hope for changing our hearts.

*"Therefore if any man be in Christ, he is a new
creature: old things are passed away; behold, all
things are become new."*
II Corinthians 5:17

Part Of My Light

∽☙☙∽

I offer you part of my light where my
poetry was born in my home tonight.

I am sharing with you my thought,
what God has laid upon my
heart to share with you.

I pray that as I share God's words with
you, you will be inspired to follow
His light.

Stay focused on God's light at all times,
and be obedient to His words.

*"I am the light of the world: he that followeth
me shall not walk in darkness, but shall have
the light of life."*
John 8:12

The Moon

Sitting here looking at the moon tonight made me think of sitting at the throne with God. The moon I saw tonight was a bright, warm, clear, full moon. It was like sitting with God at His throne. It gave me a sense of peace.

I was praising God and thanking Him too. How precious it is to be at the throne in God's arms at all times. The throne is at the top where God is.

It's amazing that God has so much power that everyone around the city can see this moon at the same time. Looking at the moon at night, you can walk around your house outside with only the light from God's throne.

God's children, how many times in your life have you just wanted to hold tight to the arms of God? When we reach out to God, He is always there for us at all times. The throne is a place where we can always go to be with God for that peace and joy in times of adversity. I can feel the presence of God looking at this moon.

"Therefore are they before the throne of God, and serve him day and night in his temple: and he that sitteth on the throne shall dwell among them."
Revelation 7:15

Light From The Moon

I feel the presence of God in my bedroom tonight.
It's dark in here, but the light from the full moon is
shining on my pillow. I can see from the moonlight
to write this tonight. I can see the moon with a
baby Angel in it, a blue circle around it, a star
beside the moon.

Looking up at the moon and seeing the light shining
on my pillow, I just want to say thank you, God, for
inspiring me to write tonight. Someone wants to feel
your power, know your peace, and have Your joy.

I thank You for the light from the moon that is
shining through my window. I can see your Angel
watching over me. I will continue to praise, praise
your Holy Name.

*"And the Angel said unto them, Fear not: for, behold, I bring you
good tidings of great joy, which shall be to all people."*
Luke 2:10

The Light From The Light Bulb

∞୫୫∞

Looking at the light bulb, what do you see?

The power of God is working through the
light bulb. The light bulb shines bright
as long as you have it turned on at the switch.

When God turns the light on in your life,
it shines bright.

You don't need a switch on the wall
to turn God's light on. Once you accept
Jesus in your life, and keep Him first,
He is your light.

Jesus gives you the light that glows within.
He gives you that peace and joy only
He can give you.

The only light you will ever need in your
life is Jesus' light.

*"The Lord is my light and my salvation; whom
shall I fear? The Lord is the strength of my life;
of whom shall I be afraid?"*
Psalm 27:1

Be Still

৯৫৩৫৩৯

Where do I go from here?

Oh God, I need to hear your voice
today, and to feel your presence.
I know you are here with me,
but sometimes I feel all alone.

Lord, you said when I feel all
alone you are carrying me in
Your loving arms.

"Be still, and know that I am God:
I will be exalted among the heathen,
I will be exalted in the earth."
Psalm 46:10

Part Three

Faith, Hope and Looking Forward To The Light

❧❧❧❧

Blood On The Cross

❦❧❧❦

God's blood ran down His body
because of the individual sins
I committed. The blood that God
shed for my personal sins was
very excruciating.

God, I love you for shedding Your
blood on the cross for me, that
I might have life more abundantly.

God, You are awesome for loving
me so much that you died on the
cross for me.

God, I love you.

"We love him, because he first loved us."
I John 4:19

Easter Morning

Oh God, Thank you for dying
for my sins and rising again
on Easter morning.

I look over the hills and see
the sun rise, and God,
I feel your presence
this glorious morning as
always, and welcome
Your loving arms around me.

I feel safe and secure, because
I know You will take care of all
the things I must endure today.

Thank you, God, for another
Easter morning.

*"But thanks be to God, which giveth us the
victory through our Lord Jesus Christ."*
I Corinthians 15:57

Microwave Life

Microwave - get it now, quick, fast, I want it now,
not later. Lord, everybody wants a quick fix.
Nobody wants to wait for anything. Lord, we are
glad you are not like us. Microwave this and
microwave that.

Our family used to sit down at the table for dinner.
We had a bond of closeness in our family. We all
knew what was going on in each other's lives.

Lord, husband and wife, family and friends don't have
time for each other any more like they used to, before
the microwave became the "fix it" for dinner time.
Microwave dinner, pocket telephone, banking machine,
talking computer.

Lord, we miss having a real dinner with our spouses,
family and friends. Sitting at the dinner table, talking,
laughing, telling each other stories of how the day went.

Thank you, Lord, for helping us to slow down, and see
the important things such as spending time with the
family and friends.

"He that handleth a matter wisely shall find good: and
whoso trusteth in the Lord, happy is he."
Proverbs 16:20

Time

❦ℬℬ❦

God, we all worry about not
having enough time each day
to do what we want to do.

There is not enough time to
work, play, spend time with
family and friends.

When I pray and thank
You each morning before I
start my day, You supply me
with the time I need.

Making time to spend with my
God is very important to me,
more than anything else in my
life. When I make time for
my God, He will make time for
me to do everything else He
wants me to do today.

*"Take therefore no thought for the morrow: for the
morrow shall take thought for the things of itself.
Sufficient unto the day is the evil thereof."*
Matthew 6:34

We All Face Obstacles

⁂

When I passed over a bump in the road this
morning, I realized why I missed my turn
onto the interstate. I was in the wrong lane
and going too fast. God was telling me
to slow down and stop rushing today.
We all have bumps in life to slow us down.

I got on the interstate further down the road. I
wanted an easy drive to work where the traffic
was running smoothly with no bumps. I realized
how my life accelerates, I run into obstacles, and
I must slow down and deal with the situation.
We must stop rushing, and ask God for help.
When the frustration comes, we will know how
to deal with the situation.

No matter what is going to happen today, God is
at the end of the road waiting for me. We must
all listen to God, and slow down for bumps in
the road.

*"For he shall give his angels charge over thee,
to keep thee in all thy ways."*
Psalm 91:11

One Said

๛๛๛๛

One said, I 'm happy for you.
One said, how much is this going to cost you?
One said, when can we go shopping.
One said, are you sure you want to write this book?
One said, why do you want to write this book?
One said, I don't like poems.
One said, I don't understand poems.
One said, call me in a couple of months, and let me know
 you are still writing a book of poems.
One said, what are you going to write about?
One said, are you going to write about Hannah in the Bible?
One said, you are a serious writer.
One said, you don't have enough experience in writing.
One said, I didn't know you could write.

I said, I can do all things through Jesus who strengthens me.

Thank you, Lord, for keeping my eyes focused on you at all
times.

"I delight to do thy will, O my God: yea, thy law is within my
heart."
Psalm 40:8

No Leftovers Here

⊰৪০৪০⊱

Thank you, God, for reminding me,
You don't want my leftovers.

No more, five minutes before I fall asleep.
No more, leftover tithes after I pay all my bills.
No more, I don't have any clothes to wear.
No more, closed mouth praising you.
No more, I don't have time to study Your Word.
No more, I, I, I . . . .
No more, excuses.
No more, No more, No more.
No more leftovers here.

"But as truly as I live, all the earth shall be filled
with the glory of the Lord."
Numbers 14:21

Fog

❧❀❀❧

I look out this window this morning
and see nothing but fog.
I can't see the building in front of me.

God, you are so powerful. It's amazing
how you have created this world
and the fog too.

God, I am lost for words.

The fog is rising from the ground.
I can see sunshine, bright and warm.
I know you are right by my side.
I feel your presence. Thank you, God,
for another opportunity to see Your work.

*"Those things, which ye have both learned, and
received, and heard, and seen in me, do: and the
God of peace shall be with you."*
Philippians 4:9

Cloudy Day

Sitting on the patio,
I looked toward the
cloudy sky.

I felt sunshine through
the clouds. Can you
imagine God sitting on
His throne looking at us
through these clouds?

Knowing my God is watching
me makes me feel good,
even on cloudy days.

"Jesus Christ the same yesterday,
and today, and forever."
Hebrews 13:8

Rain

ﾂﾟﾂﾟﾂﾟﾂﾟ

We are thankful that we have rain
to smell. The rain brings the fresh
scent of God's fragrance.

When it rains in our lives
it's for only a season,
to help us grow and
depend more on God
for our strength.

When we keep our eyes on Jesus, the
rain will stop and we will have
another season of sunshine.

*"In every thing give thanks: for this is the
will of God in Christ Jesus concerning you."*
I Thessalonians 5:18

Wind

❦❧❦❧❦

Listen to the wind blowing outside.
I can hear the wind whispering
around my house. I wonder how
it must feel to have power to make
the wind blow. Limbs on the trees
blow from side to side.

God, You are so awesome and
powerful, in everything you do.
I know I am in very good
hands when I am with You,
even when the wind howls.

I know I am safe in God's kingdom.

*"For the kingdom of God is not in word, but in
the power."*
I Corinthians 4:20

Trees Standing Tall

Trees standing tall, unbending in the wind,
remind me of God saying, "I am the vine,
ye are the branches: He that abideth in me,
and I in him, the same bringeth forth much fruit;
for without me ye can do nothing." (John 15:5)

God wants us walking with Him before the
storm comes our way.

"If ye abide in me, and my words abide in you,
ye shall ask what ye will, and it shall be done
unto you."
John 15:7

Need A Little Sunshine

Need a little sunshine today?
Just call on Jesus,
You just look around
where you are,
and begin to count
your blessings,
and you will see all the
sunshine you need today.

Call on Jesus when you are cloudy,
and He will give you all the
sunshine you need daily.

Just call on Jesus for everything in
your life each and everyday. . . .

*"I will lift up mine eyes unto the hills, from
whence cometh my help."
Psalm 121:1*

Listening To The Birds Sing

❧ℰ☙℧ℰ☙❧

Have you taken the time to ask yourself
what the birds are singing about?
Only God knows what the birds are singing.

Thank you, God, for letting me see and
hear these birds today.
Everything is important to God,
like listening to these birds sing.

I feel the power of Jesus singing to me,
Good morning, good afternoon,
how are you doing today?
Talk to me.
What's on your mind today?
Tell me.
I Love You.

*"The hearing ear, and the seeing eye, the Lord
hath made even both of them."*
Proverbs 20:12

Butterfly

❧☙☙❧

Just look at the butterfly.
You can see God's power
even in the Butterfly.
God is watching me, you, and
the butterfly at the same time.

The butterfly is insignificant to us,
but to God, he is important.
God is watching us even
when we want to fly into a new
adventure, just like the butterfly
flies into our pathway.

*"And this is the confidence that we have in
Him, that, if we ask anything according to
his will, he heareth us."*
I John 5:14

Tell God

Tell God what you are thinking
and feeling right now.
He will listen.

Are you upset at yourself or
someone for something?

Tell God all about it. He will
listen to you.

No matter what is on your mind,
tell God what's going on inside
your head and heart right now.

Stop holding it back. Tell God now.
God will listen to you.

Don't you feel better?

You see, God will not judge
you or condemn you.

God Loves You.

"Trust in the Lord with all thine heart;
and lean not unto thine own understanding."
Proverbs 3:5

My Story

◄୫୬୫◄

We all have a story to tell. Mine is the goodness
of God's love everyday. God takes us and molds
us into the person He wants us to be. God is
loving, patient and understanding toward us,
even when we say or do something that's not
pleasing to Him.

God takes us to and from church, work, home,
vacation and around the city or where ever we
want to go. Do we take the time to tell others
how good God is to us?

We take the small things for granted, but these
things are really important to God, and they
should be important to us also.

All of us have a very important story to tell
about the blessings of God.

*"I have set the Lord always before me: because
he is at my right hand, I shall not be moved."*
Psalm 16:8

Graduation

࿇ಖಖ࿇

You have traveled this road
twelve long years! Praise God,
this is your day to celebrate
your last day of high school.
Off to college, a new job,
whatever your adventures may
be, take God with you.

I can give you presents,
money, clothes to wear,
but that won't last.

The most important thing I can
give you as a gift that will
last a life time is to tell you
about my best friend,
Jesus Christ.

*"For whosoever shall call upon
the name of the Lord shall be saved."
Romans 10:13*

It's Time

❦ℰℰ❦

It's time for a wake up call
It's time for us to get off this ship
It's time to stay off the ship.
      It's Time

It's time for us to take the ship
out of our communities.
      It's Time

      It's Time
It's time to get out of our comfort zone.
      It's Time

      It's Time
To spread the Gospel of Jesus
around the world.
      It's Time

      It's Time
Are you listening to the voice of Jesus?
      It's Time

"Happy is the man that findeth wisdom, and the
man that getteth understanding."
Proverbs 3:13

Father's Day

Happy Father's Day to all the fathers.
You see, I don't have an earthly father
because he is in heaven
with my best friend, Jesus.

Even though my earthly father is not here
beside me, his spirit lives in me everyday.

Happy Father's Day to all the fathers.

"O Lord our Lord, how excellent is thy name
in all the earth!"
Psalm 8:9

Money

≪ৰ৪০৪০ৰ≫

Paying tithes and offerings is very
important to God. God wants us to
depend on Him in paying our bills,
buying groceries and whatever we
do with our money.

When we are obedient to God in paying
tithes and offerings, He said that all
our needs will be met every day. God
said He will pour out an abundance of
blessings upon us when we are obedient
to His words.

"Bring ye all the tithes into the
storehouse, that there may be meat in
mine house, and prove me now herewith,
saith the Lord of hosts, if I will not open
you the windows of heaven, and pour you
out a blessing, that there shall not be
room enough to receive it."
Malachi 3:10

God's Socket

◦❧❧◦

I can't hear my radio
without plugging the cord
into the wall socket.

You can hear
God all the time
when you plug
your heart and mind
into His socket
by studying His Word.

You will never be
left unplugged
from God's socket
when you put His Word
in your heart.

"And the spirit of the Lord shall rest upon
him, the spirit of wisdom and understanding,
the spirit of counsel and might, the spirit of
knowledge and of the fear of the Lord."
Isaiah 11:2

Check Deposited

❧❦❧❦❧

You go to the bank and deposit
your check each week or month.

Whatever the case, you trust the bank
to keep your money.

God is always willing and ready
for you to make a deposit with Him.
Study His word each day and when
you go to the bank it will say
"check deposited" with God.

God will not withdraw your check
from His account.

Have you made a deposit with God today?
Or a withdrawal from His word
to bless others with a kind word or a smile?

*"Now he that planteth and he that watereth are
one: and every man shall receive his own reward
according to his own labour."*
I Corinthians 3:8

Your Name

๑๕๐๕๐๕

Your name is very important to you.
Your name will follow you
throughout your life.
How you use it will depend on you.

Jesus' name is washed in His blood
on the cross for us.

His name is written in His book
all through the Bible for us.

Do we take the time to read
His book with
His signature on it?

Where is your name written?

. . . they shall call on my name, and I will hear them. . .
Zechariah 13:9

72

Life In The Word

There is life in the Word of God.
Put it in your heart and use it
to glorify Him.

You will always have Life in His Word
when you meditate on it everyday.

God's Word is His Life.

"One thing have I desired of the Lord, that
will I seek after; that I may dwell in the
house of the Lord all the days of my life, to
behold the beauty of the Lord, and to inquire
in His temple."
Psalm 27:4

Have Faith In God

⇛😀😀⇚

God, I know you healed me today.
There are no more pains in my body.
You are my powerful healer.
Thank you, God.

I know God moved obstacles in my
life. God can do it for you just like
He did it for me.

Whatever your fears may be, give
them all to God right now. He will
take care of you.

If you need wisdom, food,
house, car, money, healing,
or friends, go to God in prayer.
Have faith in God when you
pray and believe in Him.

Be obedient to His word at all times.

*"Trust in the Lord with all thine heart; and lean
not unto thine own understanding. In all thy ways
acknowledge him, and he shall direct thy paths."
Proverbs 3:5, 6*

Will You Be Ready When Jesus Comes Back?

❧ℰ❧ℰ❧

The President of the United States came to
Charlotte today. There was excitement
in the crowd. People of all color, all walks
of life were outside, talking and laughing,
excited to be standing on the street waiting
for a brief look at the President.

People were lined up on both sides of the
street, and on the tops of buildings, waiting
to get that brief look at the President riding
in a black car.

I asked myself, Will these same people line
the streets for a look at Jesus Christ? Jesus is
coming back for us. Will you be waiting?
We do not know the time of day, night, or
hour when Jesus will come back for us.

Will you be waiting and looking for
Jesus when he comes?

*"I am Alpha and Omega, the beginning and
the end, the first and the last."*
Revelation 22:13

Through It All

❦ℰℰℰ❦

Through it all
I learn to pray more.

Through it all
I learn to fast more.

Through it all
I learn to be obedient.

Through it all.
I learn to stay focused on Him.

Through it all
I learn to hold on to the powerful
name of Jesus.

Through it all
I learn to trust only Jesus.

Through it all
I learn to step out on Faith.

Through it all
Faith brought me through.

"For the Lord is good; his mercy is everlasting;
and his truth endureth to all generations."
Psalm 100:5

❧❦❧❦❧

I thank each of you for taking time to read
my first book. I pray that somehow, some way
this book will be a blessing in your life, and
that you will have an intimate walk with God.

*"Peace I leave with you, my peace I give
unto you: not as the world giveth, give I
unto you. Let not your heart be troubled,
neither let it be afraid."*
John 14:27

This book encourages intimacy with God
in every area of life. It offers hope,
encouragement, and most of all a best friend.

About the author:

Hannah Liles grew up in Wadesboro, North Carolina with
her parents, and five sisters and two brothers. She is a
graduate of Central Piedmont Community College in
Charlotte, North Carolina. She works in the offices of The
City of Charlotte, Department of Transportation. She is a
member of North Carolina Writers' Network. She is a
member of Nations Ford Baptist Church in Charlotte, North
Carolina, where she works with the Audio Tape Ministry.
Hannah also volunteers with Communities In Schools
mentoring programs throughout the year.

Her media exposure includes an appearance at Spirit Square
locally, and one of her poems was published in *The Charlotte
Observer* newspaper.

Be Inspired Today
Order Your Book

ᨏᨏᨏ

INSPIRED BY THE LIGHT

*Name (please print)*_____

*Address*_____

City _____

*State*_____

*Zip*_____

Sales Tax:
Please add 6% for books shipped within North Carolina.

Shipping:
# of books _____*$11.95 per book*
$2.95 shipping first book, $.75 for each additional book

Payment to: Sunflower Publishing Company
( ) check   ( ) money order   ( ) cashier's check.

Mail Payment to: SUNFLOWER PUBLISHING COMPANY
P. O. Box 240602
Charlotte, N.C. 28224

ISBN 1-890268-00-3